THE FASHION POLICE HANDBOOK

by Michelle Ironside

The Fashion Police Handbook,
©1999 Michelle Ironside

Published by arrangement of Michelle Ironside,
T.C. Publishing & Printing and
Freeman Melancon Bryant Advertising.

Library of Congress Catalog Card Number: OU812

All rights reserved, including the right to reproduce this book,
illustrations or portions thereof in any form whatsoever without prior
written consent of Michelle Ironside.

For more information book about the author or bookings,
please contact: Freeman Melancon Bryant Advertising
at 865.525.1554 or via fax at 865.525.0118

The individuals portrayed herein are fictional. Any resemblance
to a real person is purely coincidental.

A Word from the Chief

A huge challenge lies before all those who take the Fashion Police Oath. In these days of "come as you are," good dressers are harder to find than a full head of hair at a Hare Krishna Convention.

It is the responsibility of the Fashion Police Department to educate, inform and instruct the public on ways in which they can best present themselves. If we honor our Oath and uphold our mission, we truly can Keep America Beautiful.

Let's be careful out there!

The FASHION POLICE Handbook • i

Table of Contents

INTRODUCTION 2

BASIC GUIDELINES 3

Code of Ethics 8

The Oath 9

Procedures 10

Permits. 13

Commendations. 15

VIOLATIONS:

    Violation 1: Problem Underwear 16

    Violation 2: Bad Hair 23

    Violation 3: Makeup Misapplication 31

    Violation 4: Wrong Shoes. 35

    Violation 5: Improperly Contained Fat 40

    Violation 6: Delusional Dressing 46

    Violation 7: Impersonating a Prostitute 56

continued on next page

Violation 8: Earth Mother Syndrome 61

Violation 9: Unsightly Display of Flesh 63

Violation 10: Needless Display of Flesh 66

Violation 11: Clueless "Casual Day" Dressing 69

Violation 12: Unattractive Maternity Wear 71

Violation 13: Improper Accessories 73

Violation 14: Contributing to the Tackiness of a Minor ...76

Violation 15: Aiding and Abetting the Fashion Reject 79

Violation 14: Failure to Groom 81

Violation 17: Cowboy Wannabe 89

Violation 18: Fashion Rejects on Vacation 91

Violation 19: Conspicuous Mid-Life Crisis 95

Violation 20: Flagrant Display of New or Fake Money 97

Violation 21: Unacceptable Use of Tobacco Products...... 99

Questions and Answers.................................. 101

Testimonials 103

INTRODUCTION

You're standing in line at the grocery store. To your right is a woman of considerable girth sporting a pair of spandex pants, a halter top and enough makeup to cover Manhattan. To your front is a man whose toupee strongly resembles the roadkill you passed on the way to the store. In fact, everywhere you look you see another infraction. What do you do?!!

Of course, as a rookie officer it takes time to learn to deal with these issues. This Handbook is meant to serve as your guide and should be thoroughly studied and frequently reviewed so that you will be effectively prepared to deal with the fashionably challenged public you will encounter day. So, remember. Study, study, study!

It also helps to talk with seasoned officers who offer a strong support system and are able to give invaluable advice.

BASIC GUIDELINES

The offenses set forth in this Handbook are broken down into Code Names to assist officers in writing citations, making arrests, and in giving verbal reprimands to each Fashion Reject which they encounter.

Officers are required to keep this book with them at all times and should also have readily available the following items:

1. Citation Forms;

2. Fashion Police Identification Badge;

3. Laptop computer;

4. Gear bag containing shampoo, soap, a small makeup kit, large sized t-shirts, a small sewing kit, nail clippers and scissors;

5. Blow dryer and curling iron; and

6. Handcuffs.

The FASHION POLICE Handbook • 4

5 • The FASHION POLICE Handbook

FASHION CITATION

VIOLATOR

NAME: Miss IMA MISCREANT
ADDRESS: CORNER 4th and Main
CITY: Anywhere STATE: VSA ZIP: OU812
PHONE: (865) 584-3825 ☒ Habitual Offender
PRIOR ARRESTS: ☐ Yes ☐ No ☐ Frequent

VIOLATION

- ☐ Problem Underwear
- ☐ Earth Mother Syndrome
- ☐ Aiding and Abetting
- ☐ Bad Hair
- ☒ Unsightly Display of Flesh
- ☐ Failure to Groom
- ☒ Makeup Misapplication
- ☒ Needless Display of Flesh
- ☐ Cowboy Wannabe
- ☐ Wrong Shoes
- ☐ Clueless Casual-Day Dress
- ☐ F.R. Vacation Violation
- ☐ Improperly Contained Fat
- ☐ Unattractive Maternity Wear
- ☐ Conspicuous Mid-Life Crisis
- ☐ Delusional Dressing
- ☒ Improper Accessories
- ☐ Flagrant Display New/Fake $
- ☒ Impersonating Prostitute
- ☐ Contrib. to Tacky Minor
- ☐ Unaccept. Use of Tobacco

Degree of OFFENSE: ☐ Minor ☐ Moderate ☐ Extreme ☒ ARREST NECESSARY!

SPECIFIC INSTRUCTION TO VIOLATOR:
Violations are numerous and frequent - believe this one needs to be beaten with an ugly stick.

OFFICER

I, the undersigned, _Officer J Duffy_, hereby attests that he/she has reasonable grounds for issuing this citation. The undersigned further attests that he/she has counseled the violator in areas of decency and has taken all necessary corrective action at this time.

SIGNATURE OF OFFICER: _J Duffy_ DATE: 8/28/99

THE MOBILE OPERATIONS UNIT was contacted to respond immediately ☐ call cancelled
☒

At the time of arrest, the officer should take all possible steps to remedy the fashion blunder at hand, hence the need for maintaining a well equipped gear bag. In addition to taking corrective measures, the arresting officer should spend time discussing with the subject his or her fashion faux pas, offering advice and giving guidance in an effort to educate the Fashion Reject regarding how to maintain a more fashionable appearance.

Fashion Rejects will be allowed a total of five citations before they are requried to appear in front of a judge who will decide on the appropriate course of action. Those committing minor offenses will be assigned a community service project. These projects will include tasks such as finding and destroying all powder blue eye shadow or trimming nose hairs at the local park. Those unwilling to perform the community service or in continual violation of multiple codes will be arrested and required to spend time at a correctional facility.

Suspects simultaneously violating over five Codes will be detained in the Mobile Operations Unit (described more fully below) until their appearance has been improved to a point where release is permissible. Any suspect not cooperating with treatment through the Mobile Operations Unit will be arrested and taken to the nearest treatment center for a full makeover.

All citations should immediately be entered into the Fashion Police computer network, the Fashion Nanny. This will enable officers nationwide to have immediate access to a suspect's background as well as being made aware of high crime areas. The Fashion Nanny also provides an avenue for officers to share their experiences and lend moral support.

Code of Ethics

All officers shall be exceedingly courteous; they shall recognize their role as that of public servant and shall be especially attentive to civilians seeking advice or desiring to register complaints.

Officers shall be constantly aware of their surroundings, on the alert at all times, and willing to issue a citation or make an arrest whenever necessary.

Officers shall take time to educate Fashion Rejects. They shall give clear instructions and easily understandable fashion tips, offering demonstrations as necessary.

Officers shall regard their profession as a public trust and be mindful of their primary obligation, to instruct the misguided and serve the public efficiently and effectively.

Officers shall administer the law in a just, impartial and reasonable manner.

The Oath

On my honor I will do my best

to uphold the laws of fashion

I will seek out bad taste

wherever it may hide

and fight it with a passion.

Special Procedures

Fashion Police Officers should proceed based upon Special Procedures Guidelines when they are faced with an offense so hideous, a violation so extreme, or a circumstance so potentially volatile in nature that they feel unable to single-handedly manage the same.

Included in this category are what we refer to as Major Criminal Occurrences. The definition of a Major Criminal Occurrence is any incident in which the officer's safety is jeopardized or the criminal conduct requires immediate action or extensive efforts by the Fashion Police Department to resolve.

For reasons described more fully in following sections, typical violations falling under this category would include:

1. Impersonating a Prostitute
2. Bad Hair

3. Too Much Makeup

4. Improperly Contained Fat

When operating under Special Procedures Guidelines, the officer should proceed as follows:

1. Attempt to avoid confrontation and try to contain and control the situation until the arrival of additional personnel and/or the Mobile Operations Unit.

2. Notify the dispatcher of your exact location and coordinate the response of the Mobile Operations Unit.

3. Establish inner perimeter position to control and contain the escape of suspects, using handcuffs if necessary.

4. If required, the services of a negotiator should be implemented. Negotiators should be alerted in hostage situations or any incident in which their special skills could be beneficial. Negotiators are particularly useful in stopping a fashion crime before it occurs and should be

used as often as necessary in tattoo parlors, plastic surgeons' offices, and beauty salons.

5. In situations involving multiple arrests or other highly volatile situations, utilization of the Special Operations Squad (SOS) is recommended. SOS is a group of seasoned officers with considerable training in the handling of such incidents.

6. If the violations can be corrected but the arresting officer lacks the necessary tools or expertise to make the necessary modifications, the Mobile Operations Unit should be contacted. Equipped with computer imaging devices; a full service beauty salon; an alterations department; numerous articles of clothing in assorted sizes; shoes of multiple sizes and styles; and other beauty aids too numerous to mention, the Mobile Operations Unit represents the cutting edge of technology in fashion enforcement. Lovingly nicknamed the "Van 'O Beauty" by

squad members, the Mobile Operations Unit is our most powerful weapon in combating fashion blunders. Officers staffing the van have undergone extensive training in the areas of image consulting and hairstyling to further improve its effectiveness.

Permits.

Some officers may be reading this manual and wondering, "I thought this was America, land of the free. Aren't we violating civil rights?!" That's where permits come in. We on the Force are not out to stop people who make a conscious choice to look a certain way or who are following cultural traditions. We want simply to educate the uninformed or misguided and to help those unable to help themselves. Any citizen so desiring may apply for and obtain a permit to commit any of the offenses listed in this manual. Fees for permits will be charged on a sliding scale basis, with the cost for the permit increasing with the degree of unattractiveness of the offense. For example, a permit for unsightly display of flesh will cost much more than one for wrong shoes. There will be no charge for permits issued to persons who need a permit in order to accommodate a certain style for cultural or religious reasons. Once in possession of a permit, said citizen must prominently display the same on his or her person at all times so that officers will be aware of his status.

In addition to individual permits, the following permits will be granted on an at-large basis:

- All Texans are allowed to have Big Hair.

- Citizens of the state of Tennessee do not have to wear shoes.

- Citizens of New York are allowed to do most anything in the name of fashion.

- California residents cannot be found guilty of needless display of flesh.

Commendations

Officers are encouraged to issue commendations to individuals displaying a great sense of style. Commendations can be given for an overall stylish appearance or for an individual achievement, such as a good haircut, nice shoes, etc.

Commendations may also be given to individuals who have made noticeable improvements after an arrest.

Violation 1: Problem Underwear

This infraction is more difficult to police than others, as it is quite personal in nature. In order to be truly effective, however, it is imperative to start from the bottom up. With regard to Problem Underwear Offenses, Fashion Rejects need to be repeatedly reminded that underwear is meant to be worn but not seen.

Problem Panties.

Poor color selection. Darkly colored or print panties (e.g., polka dots, flowers, hearts) underneath a sheer or lightly colored outfit. Officers should instruct the Fashion Reject to purchase beige panties to be worn with such attire. Repeat offenders will be subject to a search and seizure which will result in the loss of all colored panties.

Wrong size. Generally occurring when a woman refuses to admit that her hind section has spread way beyond the boundaries of her underwear. This infraction makes one think of a Sumo wrestler because of all the extra "cheek" hanging out. If the Fashion Reject refuses to admit that she has a problem and will not purchase larger underwear, a search and seizure will be instituted and larger underwear provided in its place.

Visible panty lines a/k/a Walking Wedgie. Most common with tight blue jeans, but also seen with other attire that is too small. Painful to look at, it is hard to imagine the degree of torture these victims must be suffering from the elastic chains that bind them. Note: Do not be deceived into believing that this violation only applies to the obese. Innumerable individuals who would be considered slim or average repeatedly violate this law.

Officers encountering this offense should escort the wedgie victim into a private area and arrange for an exchange of underwear and, if necessary, new pants.

☞ **INSTRUCTION:** You know it's time to take action if the suspect is limping or bleeding.

Brassiere blunders.

Much like the panty problems, most bra mistakes occur with improper size or color selection.

Wrong size. The sizing mistake will show up in a couple of areas. The most obvious and offensive problem occurs when a Fashion Reject is wearing a bra which is too small, causing bulges of fat to ooze out around the back. The second problem area is wearing a bra that is too large, causing straps to hang out at the top. First time offenders will be let off with a warning. Repeat offenders will be ticketed and dealt with accordingly.

Poor color selection. Generally occurring when the Fashion Reject wears a darkly colored bra under a lightly colored outfit or when a white bra is worn beneath a sheer top. Again, beige is the answer. Advise the Fashion Reject to purchase a beige brassiere to be worn with such clothing.

Wrong bra. By way of example, typical Wrong Bra violations would include wearing a standard bra underneath a strapless or spaghetti strap dress or **top**, thus allowing the straps to show, or wearing a sports bra with **formal wear**. The Wrong Bra Violation is intended to include a wide range of offenses, and other violations may be cited under this Code at the discretion of the officer.

No bra. Although this violation needs no explanation, suffice it to say that if a woman's breasts are: showing through her top, sagging to her thighs, or hanging out her arm holes, she should be ticketed.

☞**INSTRUCTION:** You know there's a problem if:

- Her breasts are plagued by carpet burn

- Small farm animals follow her around **trying to get a drink**

- Her breasts are resting on the dinner table

Problem Stockings.

Stockings seem to present a particular problem for the Fashion Reject. Common problems are: poor color selection; wearing dirty nylons or those with runs in them; wearing knee-hi's with short dresses; or simply not wearing them at all. This area will require many judgment calls. For example, if a suspect claims that the run in her stockings has just occurred and she is on her way to buy a new pair, it will be necessary for the officer to decide if she is being truthful. Also, an officer will have to decide if going without stockings is not a problem with the outfit in question. In no instance, however, should a woman who is wearing a "dressy" dress or business suit be allowed to go without stockings. In general, stocking guidelines are as follows:

- No stockings that sag more than an old man's chest
- No dark "suntan" nude stockings allowed
- No black stockings with white or beige shoes
- No stockings with visible runs

- No stockings with heel marks on top of the foot
- No stockings with casual shorts or sun dresses
- Stockings should be worn with most dresses and all business suits

Officers should maintain a supply of stockings for distribution to severe offenders. Those offenders should then be fined in an amount equal to the price of three pairs of quality stockings.

Slip Infractions. Common mistakes include wearing a slip which is too long, allowing it to show at the bottom of the dress or skirt; wearing a standard slip with a slit skirt, allowing the slip to show through the slit; or wearing a frayed slip, allowing the tattered hem of the slip to show. Another problem area is those offenders who choose not to wear a slip at all when the sheerness of the dress would dictate otherwise. Slip violations are generally minor, and it will therefore be appropriate to let first time offenders off with a warning. Repeat offenders will be subject to ticketing.

Violation 2: Bad Hair

There are so many hair violations in the world today, to list them all would be an insurmountable task. This Code Section will focus on some of the most common problems. Judgment calls will be necessary with regard to offenses not specifically set forth herein.

Officers should note that all hair offenses require immediate action due to the fact that if the Fashion Reject is simply ticketed and allowed to consult with his or her own hairdresser, the problem might only be worsened. After all, the "beautician" is responsible for the damage at hand. Officers shall proceed cautiously, as many of these perpetrators are quite dangerous. If necessary, the Special Operations Squad (SOS) should be dispatched to the scene of the crime.

Unsightly color. Note that improper color selection is a recurring problem with the Fashion Reject. Hair color is certainly no exception. Whether it is the dyed black "Priscilla Presley" effect, the bleached blonde with dark brown roots, or any variation in between, prompt action should be taken. The Fashion Reject should be apprehended and escorted to the nearest salon for color treatment.

Problem perms. There are several different problem perms which need to be eradicated. One is the "poodle perm" (remember Marcia Clark at the start of the O.J. Simpson trial?); another is the "fried to a crisp" look usually occurring when hair is bleached before it is permed; another is the "growing out" perm which is seen in hair that is straight and flat on top and kinky toward its ends. Other problem perms can be cited under this Code at the discretion of the officer. All offenders should be apprehended and taken to the nearest salon for treatment. Instruction: You know the perm's too frizzy if:

- It scrapes paint off of all surfaces upon contact

25 • The FASHION POLICE Handbook

- Birds and other small flying objects continually become imbedded in it

- The makers of Brillo pads are suing for copyright infringement

Big hair. If a Fashion Reject has bangs that rise over 4" tall (obviously we are being lenient here), a water mist bottle should be used to spray the hair until the hair spray begins to lose its strength. If necessary, the bangs should also be trimmed. The Fashion Reject with an Overall Big Hairdo will be subject to a complete rinse and style. Be warned, however, it will be extremely difficult to get a comb through this type of overworked, over sprayed, and extremely teased hair. If the task is too difficult, the perpetrator should be escorted to the nearest salon for appropriate treatment.

☞**INSTRUCTION:** You know the hair is too big when:

- Christmas lights have to be strung in it to warn low flying planes
- It won't fit in a standard vehicle, so its owner is forced to drive a convertible
- While driving said convertible, the operator must pay close attention to height restrictions on bridges and overpasses
- Movie patrons have to carve holes in the hairdo in order to see the screen
- The hair has ever stopped a fly ball from making it out of the park

Rat tails. Resulting when all of the hair is cut except for one narrow portion at the base of the skull which is allowed to grow to ghastly lengths. Rat tails are not to be tolerated under any circumstance. These hideous hairstyles must be obliterated from the planet. An officer locating a Fashion Reject sporting a rat tail should remove the rat tail with standard issue Fashion Police Scissors. Be swift and silent, howeve. Anyone willing to wear such a hairstyle will likely be quite dangerous.

Ponytails on men. Rare is the man who can successfully wear a ponytail. Most men look quite ridiculous with them. If the ponytail is unattractive, it should be removed as set forth above.

Bad rug. Seen in the poor soul who thinks that he has regained his youth by wearing what appears to be a dead animal on the top of his head. All such toupees should be removed and destroyed.

☞ **INSTRUCTION:** It's definitely a bad rug if:

- The legs are still attached
- It has skid marks on it

"Swirly" Do. The swirly 'do is the hairstyle chosen by men who decide against the toupee but still desire to disguise their obviously bald state. These perpetrators allow their few remaining hairs to grow to enormous lengths, swirl them around their head, and apply an enormous amount of hair spray in a feeble attempt to create the appearance of a full head of hair.

Officers discovering these hairstyles should push the hair to one side and cut it off.

"Too" Do. The Too Do is the hairstyle that is overdone. This would include hair that is overly teased, overly sprayed, overly gelled or styled to the extreme in any manner. Officers citing this infraction should wash the hair to remove the extra spray or gel and then proceed to style the hair in a more reasonable fashion.

"Un" Do. The Un Do is the hairstyle that has never been done or has not been done in quite some time. Fashion Rejects should be detained for styling when they have any of the following maladies: shaggy hair begging for a trim, hair that looks like it hasn't been brushed for days, or hair that has been washed but not dried.

Helmet Head. This violation covers hairstyles that not only resemble a football helmet but also have the durability of one due to excessive application of hair spray. If so inclined, a person sporting this hairdo could break concrete blocks with his head. The hair should be washed (with a fire hose if necessary) to remove the excess styling agents and then restyled in a softer style.

Violation 3: Makeup Misapplication

Since the time that women rubbed berries on their lips to give them color, there has been a struggle to find the right balance between natural and repugnant. Far too few achieve that balance. Some of the most common and serious infractions would include the following:

The "Bozo the Clown" or "Tammy Faye" Look.

A very common violation, perhaps stemming from the misconception that if less is good, more is better. These vamps are certain they look gorgeous, and it is very difficult to convince them otherwise. First offenders will receive a quick makeover. Repeat offenders will be required to spend a full day at an

Estee' Lauder cosmetics counter. [Warning: Approach these violators with extreme caution. They can be quite dangerous, and are prone to "cat fights." If necessary, call SOS.]

☞**INSTRUCTION:** You know there is a problem with too much makeup when:

- Old women request her autograph and ask her if she misses Jim
- Small children are frightened by her
- She is constantly asked what it's like being in the circus
- The makeup is so heavy her head bobs forward
- She has more makeup on her shirt collar than most women wear in a week

Powder Blue Eye Shadow. After removing the eye shadow, officers should supply the Fashion Reject with a more appealing shadow color selection. In addition, the powder blue eye shadow compact should be confiscated.

No makeup. There are a fortunate few who are able to successfully go without makeup. They are, however, the exception rather than the rule. The Fashion Rejects to be cited for this violation are those splotchy skinned females under the false impression that natural is beautiful and that to apply any makeup would defile their otherwise natural glow. Obviously, nothing could be further from the truth. It is best to start out slowly with these maidens, first applying only a little base, lipstick, and mascara. We can only hope that once they see the vast improvement in their appearance they will continue to use these most needed accessories.

☞**INSTRUCTION:** You know she needs makeup if :

- She strongly resembles anyone featured in Tales From the Crypt
- She has ever been asked if her face could be used as a model for a Halloween mask
- Her skin glows in the dark

Foundation too dark. Occurring when a Fashion Reject is wearing a shade of foundation several shades darker than her natural skin tone. Special attention shall be paid to those women who have a clearly distinguishable line around the bottom portion of their chin where the makeup ends.

Fake features. Frequently occurring with women who feel the need to accentuate what isn't there. Examples would include full lips created with lip liner and smeared lipstick; large arched eyebrows created with the use of a dark pencil; and false eyelashes similar to those seen on ceramic frogs.

While the above represent extreme cases of makeup violations, officers may encounter infractions that are not so extreme but which are nonetheless irritating. Officers are instructed to use their best judgment in these instances, always bearing in mind that education on proper makeup application will greatly alleviate this plight on America.

Violation 4: Wrong Shoes

Shoe violations are as numerous as they are unsightly, and it would be impossible to clearly set forth all possible violations within the confines of this Handbook. It will therefore be necessary for officers to use their best judgment in issuing Wrong Shoe citations.

White shoes. White shoes are not to be worn before Memorial Day or after Labor Day. Do not be fooled into believing those confused souls who believe that it is acceptable to wear white shoes after Easter, and certainly don't fall for the old line that "white goes with everything." While we here at the Force would not mind seeing white shoes completely taken off the market, we are willing to tolerate them if they are clean (no black scuff marks or dirt clods on the heels), and if they are worn during summer months only. If a Fashion Reject does not conform to these guidelines, her shoes should be confiscated.

☞**INSTRUCTION:** Whie shoes worn on Christmas Day should definately be taken away.

Out of date; worn out; or other undesirable footwear. Far too many perfectly acceptable outfits are ruined by those who choose to wear them with shoes that would be better suited to a vagrant. Fashion Rejects can often be found wearing shoes that are long past their prime, with huge scuff marks on the backs of the heels, outdated styles, or overall lackluster appearance. If the problem lies with wearing shoes that simply need a good cleaning, the Fashion Reject should be directed to the nearest shoe shine stand. If a Fashion Reject is wearing shoes that have not been in style for more than a dozen years, the shoes should be confiscated and the perpetrator escorted to the nearest retail shoe outlet for a suitable purchase.

Sneakers with dress clothes. It has become a necessity

that certain downtown workers wear sneakers while they walk to and from their office. While we at the Force will reluctantly allow such a practice, we cannot be lulled into allowing the sneaky Fashion Reject to continue wearing the sneakers after arriving at the office or while running errands after work. These culprits should be ticketed, with repeat offenders losing all sneaker privileges.

Spike heels with blue jeans. Generally, the Fashion Reject who commits this violation will also be violating other codes as well. For instance, she will usually have on far too much makeup and will have either bleached blonde hair with dark roots or Big Hair. At any rate, remove the spike heeled shoes and instruct her to purchase casual shoes to wear with jeans. There are many different styles which are appropriate with jeans, so do not believe her argument that there are no such shoes to match her taste.

Platforms that reach to the sky. Platform shoes and chunky heels are the rage in fashion, and we feel we must bow to the trend and allow them to be worn. When a woman is wearing shoes that are so extremely high heeled that she is unable to walk in them, however, we must take action. If the pedestrian insists on wearing these shoes she must first apply for a permit. In order to receive the permit she must take lessons on how to balance herself and walk in these stilts. She must also provide proof of adequate insurance in the event she does not master the task.

"Pleather" shoes. Typically sold at deep discount shoe outlets and usually styled as pumps, these plastic concoctions are intended to pass for leather. The wearers of these shoes should be gently pulled aside and informed that no one is fooled and that rather than going for the 3-for-1 sale at Shoes For Less, it would be much better to invest in one nicer pair of shoes. The tackiness of these shoes is only worsened when they are dyed in colors such as bright pink, red, or lime green and worn with an outfit of identical color.

Violation 5:
Improperly Contained Fat

The Improperly Contained Fat Violation is one of the most common infractions which will be ticketed each day. Officers should be aware that this infraction is not limited to the extremely overweight. A woman weighing over 300 lbs. could be appropriately dressed and not ticketed while a woman a mere 15 lbs. overweight could be cited. The key is in containment and concealment. Officers identifying Improperly Contained Fat Violations but lacking the requisite clothing to correct the same shall immediately contact the Mobile Operations Unit indicating a special need for larger sized clothing. Any inappropriate attire should be removed (in the privacy of the van, of course) and replaced with clothing more appropriate for the individual's special needs. Note: Larger sized t-shirts are especially useful in these situations because they conceal multiple infractions and can

41 • The FASHION POLICE Handbook

be readily dispensed by officers without the necessity of contacting the Mobile Operations Unit. All officers shall maintain a supply of not less than three XXL t-shirts in their gear bags at all times for such occasions.

Typical Improperly Contained Fat Violations would include the following:

Clothing so tight that it constricts blood flow. Most often seen in jeans, but also found in t-shirts, pants, dresses and other clothing. If a t-shirt will not camouflage the problem, the Mobile Operations Unit should be contacted. The Mobile Operations Unit should make alterations if possible, with larger clothing to be dispensed if necessary. The Fashion Reject should also be measured, informed of his or her proper clothing size, and then be required to carry a card indicating that proper clothing size. The card will have to be presented before any future clothing purchases are made in order to assure that proper sizes are chosen.

Halter tops and tank tops worn by Fashion Rejects who have flabby backs and arms. Rolls of flab billowing in the wind, arms jiggling with wild abandon— it must be stopped! This violation is one which can easily be concealed with a standard issue t-shirt.

☞ **INSTRUCTION:** The arms should definitely be concealed if:

- The culprit hangs her arm out the car window and gets road burn

- She is slapped in the face with arm flesh when caught in a strong wind

Short shorts or "bike" shorts worn with extremely flabby or cellulite riddled thighs. The Fashion Reject should be given more modestly cut shorts and taken to a mirror in order to see the benefits of camouflage. If the shorts are so short that it is actually possible to see chafed skin (from thunder thighs rubbing together) an arrest will be necessary. If arrested, the Fashion Reject will be incarcerated until such time as the chafing heals and the perpetrator agrees to dress more conservatively.

☞**INSTRUCTION:** You know it's time to intercede if the suspect goes for a jog and the folks at the weather center are put on alert for earthquakes or severe thunderstorms.

Bikinis, thongs or Speedos on the obese. While it is absolutely permissible for an overweight person to wear a swimsuit in public, it is necessary that a conservative swimsuit be worn. A skimpy swimsuit draws attention to the swimmer's problem areas and may give rise to ridicule by others. A t-shirt serves as a temporary remedy for the problem, but the culprit should also be counseled on proper swimwear choices for his or her physique.

Clothing so small it allows flesh to hang out. One wonders what would possess a 400 lb. man to wear a t-shirt that would comfortably fit a five-year-old, leaving a spectacle of naked rolls of flab for everyone to view. A Polaroid snapshot should be taken of such an individual so that he will have a vivid and lasting image of how he really looks. The t-shirt should then be removed and burned and the perpetrator made to wear a shirt stating, "I've Been Busted by the Fashion Police." Note: the aforementioned t-shirts should only be distributed to the most hardened criminals. All other suspects should receive a more tasteful and attractive shirt.

Belted midriff. Women with the body type of Mr. Potato Head should refrain from wearing belts other than those which fit comfortably within belt loops. For some reason, however, many proportionately challenged women insist on stretching a belt to its very limits in order to wrap it around their swollen torsos. Fanny packs are also a favorite of these offenders and are equally unattractive. Officers should commandeer all such paraphernalia upon siting the same. Doing so will not only aid the public by improving the view but will greatly alleviate the discomfort felt by the wearers of such items.

Violation 6:
Delusional Dressing

The Delusional Dressing Violation is a very big net which catches a large number of perpetrators, a group comprised of individuals who are unable to realize how they really look in the outfit they are wearing. Representative Delusional Dressing Violations are as follows:

Wrong for the occasion. This violation causes onlookers to snicker and shake their heads in amazement. By way of example, Fashion Rejects have been ticketed for wearing the following:

1. A leather mini skirt and fishnet stockings to a christening;
2. A gold lame' halter dress to a funeral;
3. Overalls and a t-shirt to a sit-down dinner party; and
4. A linen pantsuit, dress pumps and lots of big jewelry to a picnic.

☞ <u>INSTRUCTION:</u> There is definitely a problem when the minster has to stop the service so he can regain his composure and catch his breath before continuing.

Wrong for the season. Factors to be considered are color, fabric, and style. For instance, corduroys should not be worn during warm weather months; sundresses should not be worn in the winter; and white outfits are generally reserved for summer. Exceptions would obviously apply for areas with extreme climates.

Related violations would include:

Pushing the season. This offense occurs when the Fashion Reject is overly anxious to begin wearing clothes for the coming season. Transgressions are most prominent in late winter when the sun makes its first appearance and the thermometer rises to about 45° or late August at the first cool breeze to hint at fall. In the former, the rejects throw on their short shorts and tank or halter tops; in the latter they throw away those shorts and don their woolens. Officers should contact the Mobile Operations Unit and request replacement clothing. The offenders will be much more comfortable in more seasonable attire and in late August will certainly smell much better if not allowed to wear wool.

☞ **INSTRUCTION:** You know there's a problem if:

- Visions of porcupines dance in your head when you view the person's chill bumps

- The individual's skin is turning blue or is starting to show signs of frostbite

- The suspect is sweating more than a pig at a barbecue

Hanging on to the Season. This infraction is the result of folks not wanting to let go of the clothes they have been wearing for the past six months and move on to the coming season. These are the individuals who will be seen wearing skimpy summer clothing well into fall or heavy winter apparel until summer. Persons committing this infraction should be shown a calendar and reminded that the season has changed. They should then be sent home to change into more seasonable attire.

Out of style. Apparently anxious to save a buck, or proud that they can still fit into the objectionable clothing, Fashion Rejects are often found parading about town in ensembles so outdated they nearly qualify as "retro" but are not nearly that cool. Repeat offenders of this violation will be required to donate all of their outdated clothing to a mission center. Offenders who allege lack of funding as the cause for this offense should be instructed to apply for financial aid in order to purchase more up-to-date attire.

Too Small. There are many instances when Fashion Rejects wear clothing that is too small. Some of the most common are the following:

Pants too short. Pants should come all the way to the shoes unless specifically designed to fit otherwise. We do not want to see three inches of socks, and we certainly don't want to see ugly, bare legs. In severe cases (more than 3" too short), officers should contact the Mobile Operations Unit for replacement pants.

Too tight. This offense occurs when a Fashion Reject pours his or her body into the clothing in question, leaving the appearance that if one deep breath is taken or one more cookie eaten, the zipper will lose its one remaining tooth and the entire garment will explode. If the offender is unable to laugh or blow up a balloon without explosive repercussions, the clothing should be replaced. Individuals having to unbutton their pants after eating a meal should be strongly cautioned.

Size 34" waist pants on a 40" (or more) waist. This

occurs when a male Fashion Reject continues to lower the waistline of his pants rather than purchasing larger sized trousers in order to accommodate his ever expanding mid-section. These culprits usually love to brag about the fact that they wear the same size they wore in college. Officers should pull said pants up to waist level and reveal to the Reject the ridiculousness of the situation. He should then be escorted to a men's clothing store to purchase the proper size.

Note: The reverse of this offense is when older men pull their pants up to their chest resulting in empire waist pants. Men over the age of 75 receive an automatic permit for this offense and should not be approached by officers. All others should be advised that their actual waistline is about a foot below where the pant waistline is resting and advised that they must either lower the waistline or lose the pants.

Shirts or jackets with sleeves that do not reach the wrist. This infraction makes one think of the loveable character Jethro Bodine from the Beverly Hillbillies. Hardly the look of success one would want to achieve.

Blouses or shirts with gaping holes and bulging buttons. This offense often reveals much more flesh than anyone would choose to see. Large size t-shirts are a good short-term remedy for this malady, but the perpetrator should be instructed on how to select proper sized clothing.

Suspect is wrong age to be wearing outfit in question. Many civilians have a hard time comprehending the fact that as they age they should alter their style accordingly. This is not to say that they have to dress frumpily, but simply appropriately. Country clubs across America are full of women who prefer to dress in a style similar to what they wore when they were about seven-years-old; that is, pastel, flowery dresses with lots of lace and large bows in their hair. Other women, proud that they are still a size 6, purchase their clothing in the Junior Department and sashay about in attire specifically designed for teenagers. All such women should be made to attend a one-day seminar on dressing for success. If no improvement is made, confiscation of certain articles of clothing and accessories will be necessary.

☞**INSTRUCTION:** There is definitely a reality problem if:

- The woman keeps getting her cane stuck in her ankle bracelet

- Her Depends® are hanging out of her thong

- Her hair bow has to be glued on because she has so little remaining hair

- He wants a tattoo on his rear but can't get one because no one can find his rear

Improper mixing of styles. This transgression occurs when Fashion Rejects take what might otherwise be considered appropriate pieces of clothing and put them together in freakish combinations. For instance, sneakers with formal wear; a wool sweater with white linen pants; a beaded top with wool walking shorts, etc.

Clothes that don't match. This would include improper mixing of colors and prints. While a good designer is able to make just about any combination work, Fashion Rejects are not so talented. They should not be allowed to mix odd combinations of colors, wear plaid on plaid, or mix stripes with plaid. The problems mentioned in the two above paragraphs can usually be easily remedied by the removal and/or replacement of one or two pieces of clothing.

Violation 7:
Impersonating a Prostitute

These Jezebels are truly dangerous. Convinced that they are stunning, they will be very hard to educate. The calling card of this transgressor is that of excess. As noted in the following violations, these vixens take everything to the extreme.

Too much jewelry. This would include multiple pierced earrings, rings on every finger, numerous bracelets, ankle bracelets, and toe rings. Fashion Rejects committing this violation look as if they are afraid to leave any jewelry at home, so they simply find a place on their body to put it. All excess jewelry should be removed, leaving only a few remaining pieces.

Long, long fingernails. These hideous extensions are even more unattractive when painted in obnoxiously bright colors and decorated with gold emblems such as stars and hearts.

Too much makeup. Also covered under the Makeup Misapplication Citation, this violation is the result of women applying their makeup with a garden trowel instead of makeup brushes. All makeup should be removed by whatever means necessary and fresh makeup applied in a more tasteful manner.

Too much perfume. The Fashion Reject guilty of this infraction literally bathes herself in perfume, proud of the fact that her scent lingers for hours after her departure. Allergy sufferers and those sickened by strong odors will greatly applaud all efforts at eliminating this violation.

Skimpy clothing. Women who wear excessively revealing clothing want to draw attention to themselves. What they don't

The FASHION POLICE Handbook • 58

realize is that many of the stares they receive are those of disbelief or revulsion, while most others are the leers of perverts. Standard issue t-shirts should be distributed to these violators.

Noticeable "love bites." These red marks often found on necks are the result of prolonged sucking and biting. Many teenaged girls and other misguided women actually seem proud of these marks, wearing them as a badge of honor. A little foundation should be applied to these blemishes until the same begin to fade.

Big hair. This violation is also covered elsewhere in the Handbook, but needs to be included under this section as well because it is such a prominent part of the look we are hoping to abolish.

Visible tattoos. Tattoos are becoming increasingly popular in mainstream America. Accordingly, it will not be necessary to issue citations for small, discreet tattoos. All others, however, must be outlawed. Fashion Rejects with prominently displayed tattoos, especially multiple tattoos, shall be subject to arrest.

☞**INSTRUCTION:** It is definitely time to make an arrest if:

- She can't even walk to her mailbox without being approached by "johns"

- Every time she waits for her children at the bus stop the police drive by and tell her to "move it somewhere else"

- The only hotels willing to let her rent a room charge her by the hour

Violation 8:
Earth Mother Syndrome

Earth Mothers are commonly found in health food stores, public libraries and gardening centers. They have a back-to-nature look that resists the use of anything artificial or trendy to enhance their appearance.

No makeup. For these women, going without makeup is a way of life, not a once-in-a-while necessity. The Earth Mother prefers the "natural" look, although it often requires that the rest of us view her splotchy, uneven skin.

Birkenstocks with socks. This footwear seems to be worn at all times, no matter what the occasion or the season.

No stylish clothes. The Earth Mother resists all looks

consistent with a modern-day woman. Her wardrobe consists mainly of denim jumpers, overalls and cut-off shorts.

☞ **INSTRUCTION:** Officers should intercede if she strongly resembles one of the Waltons.

Violation 9:
Unsightly Display of Flesh

Unsightly Display of Flesh occurs whenever the public is subject to viewing unattractive skin that begs to be covered. The wide variety of offenses under this violation would include, but not be limited to, the following:

Refrigerator repairman. Made a popular joke on Saturday Night Live skits so long ago, this infraction occurs when a man's pants come down so far in the back that his crack is clearly visible. The "crack" violation is a most unsightly condition which is compounded by the fact that 99% of the violators are extremely overweight. It definitely needs to be strongly policed, with repeat offenders being subject to arrest.

Sunbed to the extreme. This violation is seen in

perpetrators who have charred skin which is a strange color of brown and the texture of leather. It is easy to find this infraction because the outlaws are so proud of their "tan" that they generally wear very little clothing in an effort to show it off.

☞ **INSTRUCTION:** You know there's a problem if:

- She has to use saddle soap for lotion.
- There is no remaining white flesh on the suspect's body other the raccoon rings around his eyes

Sunburn (especially on one side). This would not include a mild sunburn, the result of a long day outdoors, but would include blazing red or pink skin, particularly when the Fashion Reject is proudly displaying the same by wearing very little clothing. This infraction is particularly unsightly when only the front or back of the body has been sunburned.

"Pasty" white skin. While it is certainly the right of any individual to choose to stay out of the sun, particularly with the threat of skin cancer, it will be necessary for this person to refrain from wearing clothing which reveals large amounts of flesh, such as short shorts, halter tops or sundresses.

Jeans with hole in the rear. Fashion Rejects need to be made aware that the public has no desire to see what lies beneath the seat of their jeans. It is unnerving enough to see underwear, but it is unbearably nauseating when bare flesh pokes through such holes.

Violation 10:
Needless Display of Flesh

Those guilty of Needless Display of Flesh violations are typically individuals who are proud of their physique and want to show it off. Although we applaud their efforts at staying fit, we have to question their judgment in choosing to wear certain attire in public.

Doing yard work in a bikini. These offenders seem to be particularly fond of yard work when there are men out in the neighborhood. They also love to bend over when cars drive by. A good public service for these women is to have them pick up roadside trash, while wearing conservative clothing, of course.

Going shopping in a leotard, skimpy exercise clothing or a swimsuit. These offenders may argue that they are committing this violation due to a tight schedule, but that is no excuse. It would take only a matter of seconds to don a t-shirt and pair of shorts before going out in public. First time offenders will be given a t-shirt. Second and third time offenders will be put on probation and required to clean the sweat from work-out equipment at the local gym. Repeat offenders will lose all skimpy clothing privileges.

Exposed midriff at office or church. This problem seems to be worsening due to the increased focus on abdominal workouts. These Fashion Rejects feel the need to show off their chiseled stomachs to everyone, forgetting all rules of decorum. T-shirts should be distributed to these individuals until an officer escorts them to a clothing store for an appropriate clothing purchase.

Violation 11: Clueless "Casual Day" Dressing

The Casual Work Day, which at first seemed to be a passing phase, has now become an increasingly important part of the work week. In fact, many businesses are going toward a more casual style throughout the week instead of limiting it to Friday. Because of the newness of this trend, multiple violations are frequently committed. It is our goal to educate these misguided employees, informing them of what is and is not proper attire for the workplace.

Worn-out jeans. This would include jeans with frayed edges, holes in them, or an overall worn and faded appearance. These suspects should be sent home to change and made to bring back donuts or other goodies for their co-workers.

Wrinkled clothing. Fashion Rejects often make the mistake of understanding casual to mean unkempt. Their clothing looks as if it has just been extracted from the depths of a laundry basket. These offenders should be made to iron not only all of their own clothing but their co-workers' laundry as well.

Tacky. Obviously a wide category, this would include clothes that are: too skimpy, out of date, or just plain ugly. Officers may cite this violation at their discretion.

Violation 12:
Unattractive Maternity Wear

Expectant mothers today have many stylish options for maternity wear. It is therefore imperative that we eliminate some of the violations which are so prevalent among the pregnant Fashion Rejects that surround us.

"Baby below" t-shirts. These ridiculous shirts are emblazoned with a huge arrow pointing toward the wearer's protruding belly. They bear the message, "Baby Below." As if we couldn't already tell.

Tight clothing. This is the result of a refusal to wear maternity clothes but instead continuing to wear regular clothing which barely stretches over the engorged body. Proper fitting maternity clothing should be distributed to these offenders.

"Baby doll" clothing. For reasons yet determined, many Fashion Rejects decide that once they become pregnant that they must begin wearing frilly, lacy clothing that would look more suitable on a Baby Tender Love.

☞**INSTRUCTION:** It's time to intervene when the expectant mother is:

- Making her clothing out of doilies
- Wearing more pink than Mary Kay
- Wearing a thong bikini the day her water breaks

Violation 13:
Improper Accessories

When properly chosen, accessories can complement and complete the look a woman wants to achieve. In the hands of a Fashion Reject, however, these items are as dangerous as a gun in the hands of a felon. Officers should remove all improper accessories, seizing those items that are extremely objectionable. Some of the more prevalent violations are as follows:

Everyday shoes/purse with formal wear. Officers frequently report citings of Fashion Rejects wearing leather flats or pumps and carrying their shoulder bags with formal evening gowns.

Junk jewelry with dressy outfits. This would include such items as plastic necklaces, mood rings, black sport watches, and other dime-store trinkets.

Big earrings. Many Fashion Rejects feel their look is not complete until they clip on a pair of earrings about the size of life preservers. Holidays seem to be a favorite time for these offenders to wear particularly large and bizarre baubles. All such earrings should be removed and replaced with a more reasonable substitute.

☞ **INSTRUCTION:** The earrings are definitely too big if dolphins can jump through them.

Accessory overload. This violation occurs when the Fashion Reject piles on jewelry and other accessories in amounts that defy logic. Often times, when all normal avenues for jewelry have been exhausted, the suspect will then begin tactics such as body piercing and piercing the ears all the way around in order to accommodate an ever expanding jewelry inventory.

Belt and suspenders. Officers should remind these Fashion Rejects that they need only one or the other. By wearing both they appear to have a phobia of losing their pants. The suspect should be required to remove one or the other.

Violation 14: Contributing to the Tackiness of a Minor

Children are a precious resource. In the hands of some parents, however, they can become unsightly creatures, annoying even the most tolerant adults. It would not be appropriate to bring charges against these innocent children. We must therefore take swift action against their parents if we want to stop the cycle of bad taste. Officers may cite parents whose children are in violation of any Fashion Police Codes. In addition, the following infractions should be cited:

Public display of diapers. A t-shirt and diaper are not proper attire for public outings. If the diaper is so wet that it hangs down to the child's knees, the officer should force a diaper change in addition to supplying some shorts to cover the diaper.

No shoes. It is not only unsightly to see these grimy feet in public, it is also dangerous to the child's safety. If shoes are not readily available, officers should contact the Mobile Operations Unit to disburse the same.

Dirty faces. While children and dirty faces go somewhat hand in hand, it is the duty of parents to remove the vast majority of grime from their children's faces before bringing them out into public. Officers should use a baby wipe or damp wash cloth to remove excess slime from the child's face.

Dirty clothing. This does not include a minor stain which is obviously the result of a recent spill, but rather the kind of filth that could only accumulate over the span of a few days. Mothers cited for the first time should be given a sample of laundry detergent and a booklet offering helpful laundry hints. Repeat offenders will be required to attend weekly sessions at the local laundromat.

Beauty pageant princess. Officers should arrest parents who, in the name of beauty, clothe their daughters in ridiculous costumes, smear their faces with huge amounts of makeup, and "foof" up their hair to ridiculous heights. Citations should be issued for parents taking their children to "Glamour Shot" photo sessions.

Violation 15: Aiding and Abetting the Fashion Reject

Much like drug dealers create an environment of crime in urban areas, these violators fuel the fires of bad taste and sacrifice all bounds of decency at the altar of enterprise. Shop owners, hairdressers, plastic surgeons and tattoo artists are all part of this circle of crime. As Fashion Police Officers, it is our duty to find these villains and thwart their efforts as much as possible.   Manufacture, sale or possession of plus-size thongs, bikinis, bike shorts or spandex pants. Obviously, no one wants to see large amounts of flesh displayed in these types of clothing. Officers discovering such items should immediately confiscate the same.

Criminally negligent hairdressing. The Bad Hair which we tenaciously pursue is obviously the result of the criminally negligent hairdresser's work. If we are truly going to make headway in stopping this crime, we must stop it at its source. All beauticians or barbers found creating the hairstyles we so abhor should have their licenses revoked and be prohibited from further hair styling activities.

Possession of a needle and ink with intent to create a tattoo. The owner/operator of a tattoo parlor who is willing to create multiple tattoos or is repeatedly cited for tattooing impressionable, clean-cut college students should be arrested. In addition, officers must routinely patrol tattoo parlors, attempting to dissuade all potential customers from defiling their skin with one of these eyesores. If necessary, a Negotiator should be called to the scene.

☞**INSTRUCTION:** A good rule of thumb as far as the number of tattoos is concerned: something is definitely out of whack if the suspect has more tattoos than teeth.

Failure to adequately perform plastic surgery. We have all seen the freaks whose looks are the result of either a botched surgery or too many trips to the plastic surgeon's office. It would be cruel to ticket individuals whose looks are already ruined. Why issue a ticket to victim who looks as if her face has been sucked off by a vacuum cleaner? It is, however, imperative that we go to the one who is truly responsible for the damage at hand — the plastic surgeon.

☞**INSTRUCTION:** Particular emphasis will be placed on plastic surgeons who:

- perform repeated face lifts

- utilize beach balls for breast implants; or

- remove more than 2/3 of a patient's nose during rhinoplasty.

Violation 16:
Failure to Groom

Whether the result of laziness or indifference, Fashion Rejects frequently fail to properly maintain routine grooming habits. Officers shall vigorously pursue such improper groomers. Nevertheless, patrolmen are instructed to grant special exceptions for senior citizens or others who may be physically unable to properly take care of themselves.

Excessive growth of facial hair on a female. This law is not aimed at a small amount of "peach fuzz," but the type of facial hair that makes young children laugh and make comments such as, "Mommy, why does that lady have a mustache?"

Instruction: Special attention should be paid to those women who have been offered a booth at the fair.

Overgrown nose hair. When a Fashion Reject looks as if a hamster is stuck in his nostrils, it is certainly time for an officer to take action and trim the same — by force if necessary.

Instruction: It's time to trim if the perpetrator's nose hairs impede his ability to eat.

One eyebrow. The result of two large, usually very bushy, eyebrows growing together and becoming one. At a minimum, tweezers should be used in order to separate the two eyebrows. It is preferable that the two resulting eyebrows also be trimmed.

Unshaven/poorly shaven legs. If a woman is wearing attire which publicly displays her bare legs, she must make sure that they are smooth. Officers should apply Nair on hairy legs or legs with large amounts of stubble. Women who choose not to shave their legs for either personal or cultural reasons will be allowed permits for the same.

☞ **INSTRUCTION:** Officers should definitely apply some Nair if:

- The woman's leg hairs resemble a mohawk

- The hairs are able to force their way through support hose or tights

- With bare legs she looks like she's wearing mohair stockings

Unshaven/poorly shaven underarms. Officers should take every effort to remedy this problem upon encountering the same. Thereafter, subjects should be required to keep a clean shave because it is so easy and takes so little time to maintain.

☞ **INSTRUCTION:** You know there's a problem if:

- Her underarms have ever been mistaken for a Chia pet
- The underarm hair is braided
- She has used a razor to carve her name or other designs into her armpit hair

Unsightly fingernails. This would include chipped nail polish; fingernails that are over five inches long; dirty fingernails; or long fingernails on a man. Officers should perform a quick manicure on these individuals.

Unsightly toenails. Similar to fingernail violations, this would include chipped polish, untrimmed, or dirty nails.

Instruction: The toenails are definitely too long if they cut through the leather on the front of the shoe.

Body odor. The only odor more offensive than the smell of too much perfume or cologne is that of body odor. Violators emitting a stench so rank that it makes those around them gag should be arrested and taken to a treatment center for cleaning and decontamination.

Bad Breath. This is not directed at a mildly offensive case of halitosis, but rather the kind of breath that makes young babies cry, that knocks you to your knees, that curls your hair. The Bad Breath violation is compounded by the fact that the individuals possessing this kind of breath are usually the ones who feel they are not properly communicating unless they are within an inch of their listener's face. One of the many fine breath fresheners on the market today should be dispensed to these felons.

Greasy hair. Stringy strands of hair hanging lifeless in a sea of oil. This particularly unsettling violation can also be worsened when huge chunks of dandruff are present. Extreme offenders should be taken to a treatment center while others shall be cited

and given a free sample bottle of shampoo.

Violation 17:
Cowboy Wannabe

Perhaps inspired by the popularity of the Urban Cowboy era during the early 1980's, Cowboy Wannabes are as common as white trash in a trailer park. Not to be mistaken with real cowboys who are not only permitted to wear western attire but who actually look good in the same, these rejects dress up in ridiculous costumes hoping to achieve a rugged, he-man kind of look that will drive the ladies wild. They drive the ladies wild, all right, with laughter.

Trademark Cowboy Wannabe Violations are:

- **Big belt buckles.** Under the misguided notion that bigger is better, these fellas wear belt buckles the size of license plates. Aside from the obvious problem with the ridiculous appearance of these oversized belt buckles, one wonders about the logistics of performing necessarily bodily functions while wearing the same.

- **Jeans (usually Wrangler) tucked inside boots.**

- **Skoal circle in back pocket.**

- **Cowboy hat worn at all times, even at the dinner table.**

- **Western shirts with elaborate embroidery and silver or pearlized snap buttons.**

Violation 18:
Fashion Rejects on Vacation

It seems that vacationing Fashion Rejects are an increasing problem. This is probably attributable to the ever decreasing price of airline tickets. At any rate, this trend requires that Fashion Police Officers stay on duty even while on leave.

Tacky t-shirts. The Fashion Reject's first vacation purchase is usually a tasteless t-shirt, often air brushed, bearing the name of the vacation spot. The Fashion Reject then proudly wears this shirt for the remainder of the trip. Equally offensive are the t-shirts brought home for the children which have sayings such as, "My Mom and Dad went to Myrtle Beach and all I got was this Stupid Shirt."

Carrying grocery bags for luggage. Fashion Rejects are

extremely fond of the plastic bags used by grocery stores and will use any excuse to carry them. When the grocery bags are used as luggage, it is obviously time for us to step in. The Mobile Operations Unit maintains a supply of clean, used luggage to be donated on such occasions.

His and Her matching outfits. Many married Fashion Rejects believe their vacation would be incomplete if they did not purchase and wear coordinating outfits. These ensembles usually go along with the theme of the trip, such as Hawaiian shirts for a beach trip, sailors' outfits for a cruise, etc.

Farmer's tan. The farmer's tan is the result of a Fashion Reject spending long hours in the sun while wearing a tank top or short sleeved shirt. When he goes shirtless, his white skin gives the appearance that he is still wearing his shirt. A t-shirt should be given to such an individual. It will not only benefit the viewing public, but will protect the perpetrator from a nasty sunburn.

Tan-in-a-bottle improperly applied. Self tanning lotion has been successfully used by the cast of Bay Watch for many years. It should be left in the hands of professionals. Amateurs who use self tanning lotion end up with multi-colored or streaked skin and orange palms. Officers should seize all self tanning lotion from these individuals unless they are willing to attend and graduate from classes offering instruction on proper application of self tanning lotion.

Shoes and socks with a swimsuit. Particularly unattractive is the man wearing dress shoes and dark socks. Flip flops should be given to such individuals.

Excessive back and body hair. These creatures create panic on the beach, causing other vacationers to think that Big Foot has made his way to the sea or a werewolf is on the loose. An Officer encountering a man suffering from a severe problem with excessive body hair should use the hair removal remedy of his choice.

☞**INSTRUCTION:** It is definitely time to take action if animal rights activists throw blood on him every time he goes topless in public.

Violation 19:
Conspicuous Mid-Life Crisis

There comes a time in every man's life when he realizes that he is not as young as he once was. Different men handle this realization differently. While we do not purport to be psychologists and definitely do not want the responsibility of analyzing the sufferers of mid-life crisis, it is our duty to cite the following violations:

Big, gold necklaces. Usually worn several at a time with a shirt unbuttoned to the navel. These chains seem to multiply as the severity of the crisis mounts. All excess chains should be removed and put away.

Hideous hair. In a futile attempt to regain their youth, victims of this disease do strange things to their hair such as greasing it with Brylcreme or other styling gels, growing it long in back while leaving it short on top (or, worse yet, bald on top), oftentimes perming the back section so that it will be curly, dying it a strange shade of black to hide the gray that has begun to creep in, or growing it long all over and holding it up with gallons of hair spray.

Too much cologne. These misguided souls have been led to believe that lots of cologne will attract women. They want more women so naturally they apply even more cologne. Bad idea. Riding in elevators or sitting near these perpetrators is especially nauseating. Any of the new air neutralizing products should be generously sprayed on these individuals.

Violation 20: Flagrant Display of New or Fake Money

Flagrant Display of New Money and Fake Money are grouped together because they are basically the same offense. The only difference between the two is that Fashion Rejects with new money are wearing the real thing and the fakers are wearing cheap copies.

Infractions include:

Excessive display of designer names. These violators are very fond of clothing that bears the name of famous designers. The larger the name and the more times it is displayed, the better.

Big jewelry, and lots of it. These rejects love to wear loads of jewelry, most of it so huge one wonders how they haul it all on their bodies. They also love to wear their biggest jewels with blue jeans and sweat suits. Excess jewelry should be removed and placed in a storage bag for safekeeping. These offenders should then be cautioned about the dangers associated with wearing so much expensive jewelry at once.

Huge purses. We are not sure what they carry in these saddlebags, but these culprits almost always carry purses big enough to conceal small farm animals. The handbags are usually emblazoned with designer initials or emblems, although some are merely gold or silver.

Violation 21: Unacceptable Use of Tobacco Products

We on the Force agree with the Surgeon General that cigarette smoking and use of other tobacco products is damaging to the user's health. However, we do not possess the authority to write tickets when citizens are properly using these substances.

Tickets should be written when any of the following occur:

Cigarettes rolled up in shirt sleeve. It is also quite unattractive to see them displayed in the front pocket of a t-shirt.

Chewing or dipping in wrong area. Chewing tobacco was never meant to be used indoors. It is definitely out of limits in restaurants, churches, offices or movie theaters. All suspects apprehended while chewing or dipping in these areas should be made to swallow their "wad." This is guaranteed to serve as a great deterrent to such behavior.

Cigarette hanging out of mouth. There are few things more unattractive than a woman with a cigarette limply hanging from her tar-stained lips. All such limp cigarettes should be flipped out of the user's mouth and snuffed out by foot. The smoker should then be made to pick up and properly dispose of the snuffed out cigarette.

Smoking outside building in outrageously inclement weather. It would seem that these smokers could be cited for sheer stupidity, but we lack the authority for writing such tickets. These suspects will inevitably be in violation of other codes, however, after standing in rain, hail, sleet or snow in order to grab a few puffs. Officers should be ready to fix hair, reapply makeup and repair torn or muddy clothing at these times.

Questions and Answers

Q: **Is it ever OK to pull someone over in their car?**

A: Yes. Although on-the-road arrests should be kept to a minimum, an officer citing an extreme violation is authorized to take such an action. For example, if the hair is so big that it fills up the entire car, a pull-over would be allowed.

Q: **Can you give me an example of a "good" encounter with a suspect?**

A. Of course. Suppose it is mid-October. An officer walks up behind a woman who is wearing an attractive fall dress with a pair of white leather pumps. The officer could say something as follows: "Excuse me madam, [while flashing police identification] I'm a Fashion Police Officer. That's a lovely dress you're wearing, but I'm afraid it's too late in the season for white shoes. Perhaps you could try something beige next time."

Q: What if I'm at a ball game or the fair? It seems that there are too many offenses to even consider taking them on.

A: Good point. At times like these you must take as many immediate steps as you are able, but your first priority should be to call the Special Operations Squad for backup. While waiting for the additional units to arrive, focus on the bigger infractions, leaving the smaller ones behind. For instance, it would be far better to cut off three rat tails than to have 20 arrests for wrong shoes.

Testimonials!

"I had the worst perm you could ever imagine. My hairstyle looked like that of a poodle gone wild. Thanks to an arrest from the Fashion Police, I now have a wonderful coiffure and am accepted by the public."

-- M. Clark, California.

"I used to love to go around without a shirt so the ladies could see all the tattoos on my mammoth body, but now I'm afraid to because those danged Fashion Police Officers are always around."

-- B.A., Alabama.

"I was always proud of my big hair and tons of makeup, why it even attracted some men in very high places, but now that I keep hearing about the Fashion Police I'm starting to wonder if I should change my style."

-- P. Jones, Arkansas.

"At the store where I worked, we were forced to lie to our customers in order to keep up sales. I remember telling a 250 lb. woman that she looked fabulous in a thong leotard that looked like it would explode if she did a jumping jack. Thanks to constant patrols from the Fashion Police, the store manager no longer allows us to make those kinds of fraudulent sales."

-- B.S., Ohio.

"One day I was at the grocery store with my Mommy when a nice lady with a badge gave my Mommy a ticket. She said I shouldn't have a rat tail, I needed to clean my face, and I should lose the ear ring. Now that I'm cleaned up, my second grade teacher is much nicer to me."

-- P.W.T., Georgia.

"I used to spend all my money going to the suntan parlor. I thought if I was dark enough I would look youthful and sexy. Since I was arrested, I have enough money to play Bingo every night of the week and can still afford to buy candy for my grandchildren."

-- C.K., Tennessee.

NOTES:

NOTES:

The FASHION POLICE Handbook • SUPPLEMENT

FASHION CITATION

VIOLATOR

NAME _____

ADDRESS _____

CITY _____ STATE _____ ZIP _____

PHONE (_____) _____

PRIOR ARRESTS: ❑ Yes   ❑ No   ❑ Frequent   ❑ Habitual Offender

VIOLATION

❑ Problem Underwear   ❑ Earth Mother Syndrome   ❑ Aiding and Abetting
❑ Bad Hair   ❑ Unsightly Display of Flesh ❑ Failure to Groom
❑ Makeup Misapplication ❑ Needless Display of Flesh ❑ Cowboy Wannabe
❑ Wrong Shoes   ❑ Clueless Casual-Day Dress ❑ F. R. Vacation Violation
❑ Improperly Contained Fat ❑ Unattractive Maternity Wear ❑ Conspicuous Mid-Life Crisis
❑ Delusional Dressing   ❑ Improper Accessories   ❑ Flagrant Display New/Fake $
❑ Impersonating Prostitute ❑ Contrib. to Tacky Minor ❑ Unaccept. Use of Tobacco

| Degree of OFFENSE | ❑ Minor | ❑ Moderate | ❑ Extreme | ❑ ARREST NECESSARY |

SPECIFIC INSTRUCTION TO VIOLATOR:

_____
_____
_____
_____
_____
_____
_____

OFFICER

I, the undersigned, _____, hereby attests that he/she has reasonable grounds for issuing this citation. The undersigned further attests that he/she has counseled the violator in areas of decency and has taken all necessary corrective action at this time.

_____   _____
SIGNATURE OF OFFICER   DATE

❑ THE MOBILE OPERATIONS UNIT was contacted to respond immediately   ❑ call cancelled

The FASHION POLICE Handbook • SUPPLEMENT

FASHION CITATION

VIOLATOR

NAME _____

ADDRESS _____

CITY _____ STATE _____ ZIP _____

PHONE (_____) _____

PRIOR ARRESTS: ❏ Yes ❏ No ❏ Frequent ❏ Habitual Offender

VIOLATION

❏ Problem Underwear	❏ Earth Mother Syndrome	❏ Aiding and Abetting
❏ Bad Hair	❏ Unsightly Display of Flesh	❏ Failure to Groom
❏ Makeup Misapplication	❏ Needless Display of Flesh	❏ Cowboy Wannabe
❏ Wrong Shoes	❏ Clueless Casual-Day Dress	❏ F. R. Vacation Violation
❏ Improperly Contained Fat	❏ Unattractive Maternity Wear	❏ Conspicuous Mid-Life Crisis
❏ Delusional Dressing	❏ Improper Accessories	❏ Flagrant Display New/Fake $
❏ Impersonating Prostitute	❏ Contrib. to Tacky Minor	❏ Unaccept. Use of Tobacco

Degree of OFFENSE: ❏ Minor ❏ Moderate ❏ Extreme ❏ ARREST NECESSARY

SPECIFIC INSTRUCTION TO VIOLATOR:

_____
_____
_____
_____
_____
_____
_____

OFFICER

I, the undersigned, _____, hereby attests that he/she has reasonable grounds for issuing this citation. The undersigned further attests that he/she has counseled the violator in areas of decency and has taken all necessary corrective action at this time.

_____   _____
SIGNATURE OF OFFICER   DATE

❏ THE MOBILE OPERATIONS UNIT was contacted to respond immediately ❏ call cancelled

The FASHION POLICE Handbook • SUPPLEMENT

FASHION CITATION

VIOLATOR

NAME_____

ADDRESS_____

CITY_____ STATE_____ ZIP_____

PHONE (_____) _____

PRIOR ARRESTS: ❏ Yes ❏ No ❏ Frequent ❏ Habitual Offender

VIOLATION

❏ Problem Underwear	❏ Earth Mother Syndrome	❏ Aiding and Abetting
❏ Bad Hair	❏ Unsightly Display of Flesh	❏ Failure to Groom
❏ Makeup Misapplication	❏ Needless Display of Flesh	❏ Cowboy Wannabe
❏ Wrong Shoes	❏ Clueless Casual-Day Dress	❏ F. R. Vacation Violation
❏ Improperly Contained Fat	❏ Unattractive Maternity Wear	❏ Conspicuous Mid-Life Crisis
❏ Delusional Dressing	❏ Improper Accessories	❏ Flagrant Display New/Fake $
❏ Impersonating Prostitute	❏ Contrib. to Tacky Minor	❏ Unaccept. Use of Tobacco

Degree of OFFENSE ❏ Minor ❏ Moderate ❏ Extreme ❏ ARREST NECESSARY

SPECIFIC INSTRUCTION TO VIOLATOR:
_____
_____
_____
_____
_____
_____
_____

OFFICER

I, the undersigned, _____, hereby attests that he/she has reasonable grounds for issuing this citation. The undersigned further attests that he/she has counseled the violator in areas of decency and has taken all necessary corrective action at this time.

_____   _____
SIGNATURE OF OFFICER   DATE

❏ THE MOBILE OPERATIONS UNIT was contacted to respond immediately ❏ *call cancelled*

The FASHION POLICE Handbook • **SUPPLEMENT**

FASHION CITATION

VIOLATOR

NAME _____

ADDRESS _____

CITY _____ STATE _____ ZIP _____

PHONE (_____) _____

PRIOR ARRESTS: ❏ Yes ❏ No ❏ Frequent ❏ Habitual Offender

VIOLATION

❏ Problem Underwear	❏ Earth Mother Syndrome	❏ Aiding and Abetting
❏ Bad Hair	❏ Unsightly Display of Flesh	❏ Failure to Groom
❏ Makeup Misapplication	❏ Needless Display of Flesh	❏ Cowboy Wannabe
❏ Wrong Shoes	❏ Clueless Casual-Day Dress	❏ F. R. Vacation Violation
❏ Improperly Contained Fat	❏ Unattractive Maternity Wear	❏ Conspicuous Mid-Life Crisis
❏ Delusional Dressing	❏ Improper Accessories	❏ Flagrant Display New/Fake $
❏ Impersonating Prostitute	❏ Contrib. to Tacky Minor	❏ Unaccept. Use of Tobacco

Degree of OFFENSE   ❏ Minor   ❏ Moderate   ❏ Extreme   ❏ ARREST NECESSARY

SPECIFIC INSTRUCTION TO VIOLATOR:

_____
_____
_____
_____
_____
_____
_____

OFFICER

I, the undersigned, _____, hereby attests that he/she has reasonable grounds for issuing this citation. The undersigned further attests that he/she has counseled the violator in areas of decency and has taken all necessary corrective action at this time.

_____   _____
SIGNATURE OF OFFICER   DATE

❏ THE MOBILE OPERATIONS UNIT was contacted to respond immediately   ❏ call cancelled